LIFE LESSONS FROM
YOUR CAT

WE'RE SO VAIN,
WE PROBABLY THINK
THIS BOOK IS ABOUT US

ANTHONY RUBINO JR.

THOMAS NELSON
Since 1798

NASHVILLE   DALLAS   MEXICO CITY   RIO DE JANEIRO   BEIJING

Published in Nashville, TN, by Thomas Nelson. Thomas Nelson is a trademark of Thomas Nelson, Inc.

Thomas Nelson, Inc., titles may be purchased in bulk for educational, business, fundraising, or sales promotional use. For information, please e-mail SpecialMarkets@ThomasNelson.com.

Illustrations by Anthony Rubino Jr.

Library of Congress Cataloging-in-Publication Data
Rubino, Anthony, 1966–
  Life lessons from your cat : we're so vain, we probably think this book is about us / Anthony Rubino, Jr.
      p. cm.
  ISBN-13: 978-1-4016-0342-7
  ISBN-10: 1-4016-0342-4
  1. Cats—Humor. I. Title.
PN6231.C23R83 2007
818'.602—dc22

2007007607

Printed in the United States of America
07 08 09 10 11 — 5 4 3 2 1

TO ALL OF YOU with furry, narcissistic companions. Without you people, I'd have no friends. And you're probably good with cats, too.

SPECIAL THANKS

Special thanks go to Sylvester (the cat, not the Stallone) and the great Mel Blanc, Friz Freeling, and Chuck Jones.

Thanks also to my editor, Jennifer Greenstein; and my agent, Jim McCarthy; and to Bryan Curtis for getting the party started.

Once a bad ol' putty tat,
always a bad ol' putty tat.
—TWEETY BIRD

Cats always seem so very wise,
when staring with their half-closed eyes.
Can they be thinking, "I'll be nice,
and maybe she will feed me twice?"
—BETTE MIDLER

Support your local ASPCA:
www.aspca.org

Adopt a cat:
www.americanhumane.org

Foster a cat: www.littleshelter.com

INTRODUCTION

So I'm having this deep conversation with my cat the other day . . . and I'm going on and on about all my problems. I told my cat that my car was in the shop again—I told her that my boss is a jerk, and how I'm sick and tired of the weather, and that I lost my cell phone again, and, oh yeah . . . I think I've got a cold coming on, and by the way, for some reason my butt is killing me. "Life's a drag sometimes, Cleo," I said. "Ya know what I mean?"

But Cleo the cat just rolled over on her back and looked at me with this expression that said, *I have no idea what you mean, and by the way, you hairless ape . . . scratch my belly.* And it was while I was scratching my cat's belly that I realized the reason my butt hurt was because I was sitting on the floor so that Cleo could have more room on the couch.

While I was leaning over to allow my left buttock to take some of the pressure from my right I said to my cat, "Hey, why is it that you're the one all comfy and content and I'm the one with all the problems, sitting on the cold hard floor?"

Cleo had no answer for me, however, because she was no longer there.

That was when it hit me. No, not the idea for this book—not yet. The lamp hit me—on the head—because Cleo knocked it over during her frenzied bolt to the chair for no discernable reason.

As I cleaned up the broken bulb and watched my cat, who was absently shredding the cushions of my favorite chair, the imbalance in our human/cat relationship became apparent. It was all too clear that we humans are *not* the superior of the two species. Did I have a cat, or did my cat have me?

I stood there with my ruined bulb in a dustpan and thought, *Isn't it telling that while our cats are content, we are confused and concerned? While they are at peace, we are perturbed and perplexed? Our lives take us down a meandering, bumpy path of distractions and distress; meanwhile our cats are making a feline beeline to happiness. Let's face it—our cats wind up with the lion's share of life.*

It was then that I realized that my feline is *way* smarter than me. Armed with the new revelation that I am nowhere near as intelligent as a twelve-pound quadrupedal feline with a brain the size of a walnut, I was unburdened! I was free to turn to our feline brothers and sisters and ask for their help. And that is exactly what I did.

I embarked on a quest for cat knowledge the likes of which has not been seen since Tweety got inside Sylvester's head (figuratively *and* literally as it turned out in "Birds Anonymous," Warner Bros., 1957). I interviewed big cats, little cats, skinny cats, fat cats, black cats, inside cats, outside cats, Cat Stevens, and Katarina Witt on a catamaran in Katmandu. OK . . . not so much that last part. Look, the point is, I embedded myself in the fuzzy folds of cat culture, mining for rich nuggets of cat philosophy. Yes, I became one with the creature we call *kitty*.

Here on the following pages—coughed up for all of mankind, like so many hairballs—are kernels of cat wisdom. Our precious felines finally have a voice. And that voice resonates in this book: *Life Lessons from Your Cat*—an in-depth look at the advice our cats would give to us if they could speak, as well as the advice they would give to their feline colleagues and peers.

So curl up in a patch of warm sunlight, turn the page, and you'll soon discover that the cat no longer has the cat's tongue.

The difference between cats and dogs: sometimes dogs believe they're human. Cats never slum it like that.

If you are unmotivated, lethargic, listless, prone to wild mood swings, and have a sporadic appetite, you are either a depressed person or a very happy cat.

Never put off until later the nap
you could be taking right now.

Do unto others as you feel like it.

I'll take it easy on the catnip
when you take it easy on the Merlot.

How was I supposed to know you
only got up to use the bathroom and
that you'd want your spot back?
My brain is, like, the size of a walnut!
Now, sit over there.

A watched can never opens.

Just ignore all those people who think cats have it so easy. Unbridled apathy takes a lot out of you.

Cats may have short attention spans,
but at least we . . . squirrel!

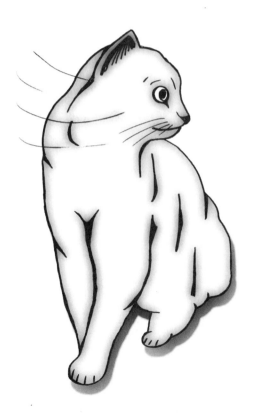

Cats can be a little moody. So it's important to show your people you really do love them by sleeping on their heads.

Sure . . . those might be your person's feet under the covers and *not* "blanket mice," but do you really want to take that chance?

In most cases the "Who me?" look will do. Save the "Who moi?" look for when furniture damage is involved.

Breakfast:
One bed pounce and a loud howl.

Cat treat:
A well-timed nuzzle and two meows.

Tuna salad left unattended
when she answers the phone:
Priceless.

Another difference between dogs and cats: if Lassie were a cat, all those times they asked her to "get help," she would have gone for therapy.

If the mice are at play when you're not away,
then you need to work on your motivational skills.

You can't teach an old cat new tricks. But then you can't teach a young cat new tricks either . . . so . . . you know . . . get a dog if tricks are your thing.

It's just not true that we want you all to ourselves. We know you need romance in your life. So when you find that special someone, we'll let you know.

Let the sun come to you.

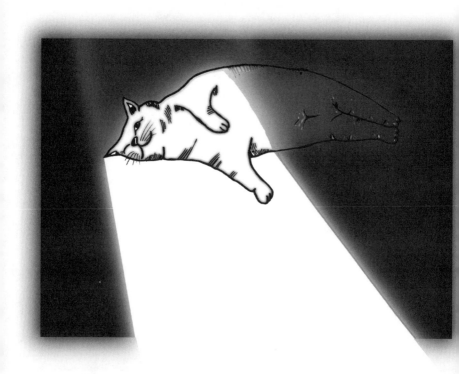

Thou shalt have
no other pets before me.

Nothing says "I love you"
like a freshly killed rodent.

Bird watching is a great hobby.
Especially watching them from some
nearby tall grass . . . crouched down
low and creeping up behind them
reeeeeeal quietlike.

One good turn gets most of the covers.

Really? Staring is rude? And what is eating the best parts of a giant fish in front of an instinctual carnivore with extremely sensitive olfactory glands? *Polite?*

Don't bother us with trivial matters
when we're in the throes of calamity!
Can't you see my rubber mouse just
rolled under the cabinet?!
This is a *disaster!*

Don't do the crime if you can't do the time . . . or just frame the dog.

Think outside the litter box.

It's strange that people are amazed
at our ability to "enjoy the moment."
What else is there?

Cat toys are great, but I'm just as happy with some yarn or a shoelace. I mean, I need another rubber mouse like you need another cat book.

There's finicky—and then there's too finicky.

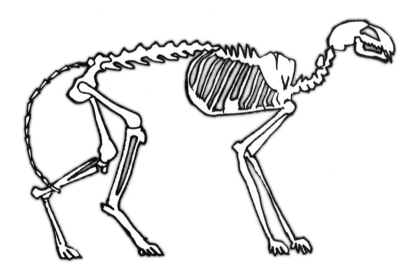

When I start coughing up balls of *your* hair, you might want to start thinking about a toupee.

You know we're just messing with you when we hide under the bed and surprise you by swiping at your foot, right? Kind-a like when you keep that piece of string just out of our reach. Touché, my friend . . . touché.

I'm in love with your blue wool socks!
There, I said it! Now just leave us alone!

Distrust the lactose intolerant.

If there's a dog in both yards, sitting on the fence is not indecisive. It's prudent.

Cats will never pretend to like something. See! That's one less thing you have to worry about. You'd be crazy *not* to have a cat.

A hiss by any other name is still a hiss.

We don't *want* to stare at you while you're having sex. But it's like a traffic accident! We just can't look away no matter how hard we try.

Hey . . . we can't stay kittens forever . . . and we had some good times, you and me, when I was younger. But listen . . . things change. People and cats move on. So maybe we're just friends now . . . it's not you . . . it's me.

Be the alpha being.

When in doubt, groom.

There's nothing like warm laundry
on a cold day.

Sometimes it's not a fur ball, ya know. Sometimes we're just clearing our throat so you'll get the heck out of our way.

Got milk?

Personalize your space. Put a knickknack here—spray a little urine around—a few dead rodents there . . . you'd be surprised!

Too much of a good thing
is a better thing.

Wᴍ

You scratch my back; I'll scratch your
hand if you stop scratching my back.

You know what you call a joint with one litter box and three potted plants? A four-bathroom apartment.

It's *ketchup,* not *catsup.*

Being a cat means you never have to
say you're sorry—unless you want
something.

Smarty, Foo Foo, Iggy, Stinky,
Spot, Smiley, Mr. Pippin, Wee Wee,
Mercedes, Beamer, Moo Moo, Dinky,
Speckles, Tiger, Honey, Garfield,
Heathcliff, Felix, Stan, Kiki, Sweetheart,
Smoochie, Greg, Misses Wiggly,
Poo, and Tinkles. Yeah . . . don't
name us that.

The right collar can be quite slimming.

This may surprise you, but I think certain people should have dogs instead of cats. People with lots of rocking chairs, for example.

When the moon hits your eye like a big pizza pie, get up on a fence and yowl.

If you'll just give me exactly what I want the second I want it, I wouldn't *need* instant gratification.

Have you ever woken up and thought it was the weekend, but it turned out to be a weekday and you had to go to work? Yeah . . . there's no life lesson here, I'm just sayin' . . . that must suck for you.

Consider not neutering.
Kittens make great holiday gifts!

The farmer's wife *rocks!*

It's not that cats are self-centered and indifferent . . . OK . . . yeah, it is.

Don't get caught up in whether you're a "mixed breed" or "full breed" like some people do. Who died and made *them* "Best in Show"?

Leap first. Worry about
sticking the landing in midair.

Watch out, because people often contradict themselves. The same old lady who complains about animal cruelty insists on calling you "Mr. Tinkles."

People want you to eat what you're served, go in the kitty litter, and stay off the furniture. So, go easy on them. Their lives are filled with disappointment.

If lovin' twine is wrong,
then I don't want to be right.

Being a cat means you don't have to come when you're called. But you really should take a message and get back to the person later.

If cats could talk, we wouldn't.

There's always time for a quickie.
Naps! I'm talkin' about *naps!*

If you wait for the third bowl of food before you start getting finicky, you may be workin' on a weight problem there, Fluffy.

People can be selfish. I mean, you lay right across the keyboard, so that it's super-convenient for them to stop typing and pet you, and they act like you're not doing them a favor.

A group of kittens is a *kindle*. A group of adult cats is a *clower*. A group of teenaged cats is nothing but trouble.

Oh, stop with the indignant looks already!
Like you wouldn't lick yourself there if you could!

Man is dog's best friend.
OK—*whatever*.

Where there's a will, there's a way
to get stuck in a hanging plant.

Sure, people get upset when you wake them up. But don't blame yourself! It's not *your* fault they're so boring when they're asleep.

Despite what you see on TV, mice rarely have perfectly arch-shaped adobe-style doorways.

Cats may seem pompous and self-absorbed, but that's only because we're so pretentious and uppity. Wait . . . that didn't come out right.

If you get upset when your person touches your tail and then the next day you like it when they touch your tail, they're going to wonder why you're messing with their heads like that. Excellent! Your job is done.

Pay attention. I mean, exactly what part of
meow don't you people understand?

Just say no to catnip.

Why climb the curtains?
Because they're there.

Experts say that cats lick their fur right after you pet them because we're using our sense of taste to get to know you. Um . . . OK . . . yeah . . . we're not just trying to lick your stink off us . . . or anything like that.

When cornered, bow your back and stand your ground, and that bully just might back down. If that doesn't work, scratch his eyes out.

The allergic are dander if they do and dander if they don't. Just a little cat humor . . .

You can please some of the people some of the time, and you can please all of the people some of the time, and you can please some of the people all of the time . . . and you—oh man! See, this is why we never try to please anybody ever. It's exhausting!

Cats have plenty of ailments to worry about, but insomnia isn't one of them.

Have you ever done something you shouldn't have—that made your person mad—and then felt bad about it? Yeah . . . me neither.

A cat's age isn't what it used to be. They say these days that your "ninth life," is your new "eighth life."

Could be a "come hither" look we're giving you.
Could be gas. Good luck with that!

Shed *toward* the velvet slacks—
never *away.*

We're so vain, we probably think
this book is about us.

People make a big fuss when you unravel the entire roll of toilet paper. Well, if you can think of a way to spin that thing for . . . like . . . five minutes *without* unrolling it, I'd like to hear it.

People say that a thousand years ago cats were worshiped as gods. That implies this is no longer the case. Aren't people *cute* when they're in denial?

Speak in high-pitched friendly
tones when you want your cat to
obey you. It won't do you any
good, but it's entertaining.

When you discover that your cat has scratched up the furniture or broken something, take a deep breath and count to ten before you act.

When a person discovers that you've scratched up the furniture or broken something, run like heck while they're counting to ten.

Of course we look up to you.
We're only as tall as your calf.

LAWS OF CAT PHYSICS

An object in perpetual motion tends to stay in motion. An object at perpetual rest tends to be a cat.

A cat in motion tends to stay in motion unless acted upon by the warm indentation your butt leaves on the couch when you get up to get some ice cream.

The distance between the countertop and the kitchen table is exponentially equal to the force necessary to prevent you from sliding off and taking the tablecloth with you.

$$E = M I C E^2$$

The shortest distance between two points is a straight line. The shortest distance between the living room and the electric can opener is a feline.

Respect children and the elderly. Both are
likely to accidentally feed you twice.

Breeders like to watch. 'Nuff said.

If God had wanted us to care,
he would have made us dogs.

Some women get upset if they have to leave the house with cat hair all over them. I don't know what they're complaining about. Haven't they ever heard of accessorizing?

Why run and fetch when you can lie and stretch?

Cats don't celebrate the Fourth of July. It's not because we aren't patriotic. It's just that it would be redundant. Every day is Independence Day—isn't it?

There are seven deadly sins. Cats have nine lives. That's all the math you need to know.

Black is beautiful all the time—
not just on Halloween.

If at first you don't succeed—try
to make it to the counter from the
armoire again.

People have screwed-up priorities.
They say stuff like, "If you're not careful
the world will pass you by." Like that's
a *bad* thing?

Soap is redundant.

Don't be intimidated by those hoity-toity full breeds who think they're all that. They cough up hair one clump at a time, just like the rest of us.

Cats—the original document shredder.

All work and no play makes you
a . . . well . . . a human.

Give us five minutes alone with the parrot
and we'll make him sing like a canary.

Work very hard at resting.

No use cryin' over spilt milk.
It's *much* easier to get to that way.

Let the buyer beware. Even free kittens come with a catch. Those things grow up to be cats, ya know.

When someone tells you to "get down" they probably want you to get off of a piece of furniture or countertop. It rarely means you should get up and start dancing.

It's important to find a reliable place for "alone time." Somewhere quiet, where you won't be bothered—a bedroom . . . a cozy den . . . a breakfast nook . . . the inside of a clothes dryer . . . something like that.

Doggie style isn't just for dogs.

A pounce of prevention is worth
a ton of prevention.

We may not be interested in what you're serving for dinner, but it's nice to get an invitation just the same.

Loathe and love unconditionally.

♕

Don't be fooled. Real mice
rarely have bells in them.

Running as fast as you can and then climbing up the nearest curtain is—unfortunately—not the answer to *all* of your scary problems.

Don't take our frequent yawning to mean we're bored all the time. We're bored all the time whether we yawn or not.

They watch you go to the bathroom.
You watch them go to the bathroom.
It's disturbing but fair.

Focus with extreme and laser-like intensity on the task at hand until you are distracted by a wiggly string or jingly little bell. Then abandon what you're doing and focus with extreme and laser-like intensity on that.

Don't jump at opportunity. Pounce at it.

Let us prey.

Don't be concerned that you only
have one name—works for Cher.

Always remember: home is where the heart is—and the liver and the kidneys and hoofs and whatever else they put in cat food.

People think we're apathetic, but in our defense
we don't really care what people think.

Today: Nap, play with a shoelace, have some food in a bowl, stretch, yawn, nap, stare at the fish, and nap.

Tomorrow: Play with a shoelace, *then* nap, have some food in a bowl, stretch, yawn, nap, stare at the fish, and then nap again. You know . . . keep it interesting.

If a glass falls in the kitchen and there is no one there to hear it—blame the dog.

If you love something, set it free. If it comes back, it's yours. If it doesn't come back—stalk it and kill it.

People say "You are what you eat."
Oh man, I hope not.

We're not playing "hard to get."
We *are* hard to get.

Cleanliness is next to godliness.
Godliness is next to fluffiness.

If you're one of those cats that use the toilet, be careful you don't lose your balance. I once knew a short-haired tabby with an inner ear infection and . . . well . . . let's just say he would have been better off using the cat box . . . may he rest in peace.

Don't play favorites. Ignore everyone equally.

Purchase comfortable furniture. I mean . . . what's the point of having an armoire that you can't take a nap on?

You stroke my belly and I'll stroke your ego by letting you stroke my belly. It's a win-win.

Stay away from Korean restaurants—trust me.

Have respect for all the creatures on
the earth—that are bigger than you are.

Why beg when you
can strongly suggest?

Going up a tree is optional.
Coming down is not.

If you doubt that cats are smarter than dogs, then wait . . . let me guess . . . you're a dog.

The truth shall set you flea.

It's normal for a cat to get jealous when a woman is having a baby. We're not jealous of the baby though. We're jealous because you don't have to have, like, *eight* babies at *one time*!

Do your part to make guests feel welcome by accompanying them into the bathroom. You don't have to do anything. Just sit there and stare at them while they relieve themselves.

Having a dog is like putting a flea collar on a hairless cat. What's the point?

Give blood. Adopt a cat.

Live every life like it's your ninth.

We're here! We're nonpedigree!
Get used to it!

They say you can't train cats because we don't understand commands. Um . . . OK . . . whatever gets you to sleep at night.

It's hard to think about, but you really need to get your affairs in order and draw up a will. You know, so the little details don't get overlooked—stuff like where you want to be laid to rest, the type of service you want, whether to leave your estate to your rotten kids who never visit and don't deserve a cent, or to . . . oh . . . I don't know . . . a beloved pet who's not the dog. That sort of thing.

You know how sometimes it's just overwhelming
to be so beautiful? Well . . . of course you don't.
How could you?

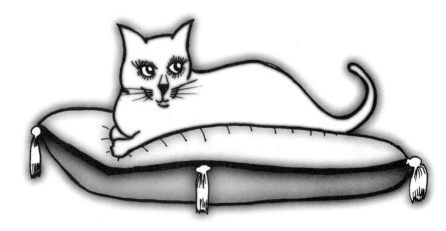

Always follow the rules . . . in your head.

Go out on a limb for birds. Literally.

Can't sleep at night? Make a bunch of noise.
Then you'll at least have some company.

Shoot for prom queen,
settle for drama queen.

It's not that we don't care. It's just
that we're indifferent to everything.

Let's call a spade a spade here. The "clumping" kitty litter is for *you*, not *us*.

Climb fast and high. That's what
the fire department is *for*.

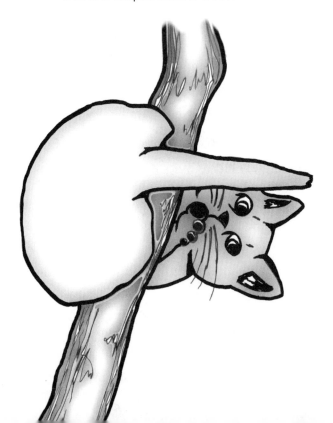

If you'd just get furniture, carpeting, and drapes that match your cat's fur, then the shedding wouldn't be a problem, now would it?

There is no such thing as a free kitten.

If you can't be with the one you love,
breed with the one you're with.

Stalk the meek.

Practice random acts of mayhem.

"Don't lose any sleep over being a good cat" is a good example of an oxymoron.

Rules are like curtains. You don't know exactly what they're made of until you rip them to shreds.

Watch for subtle hints that
your cat wants to go out.

For whom does the can opener toll?
It tolls for thee.

No situation or problem is ever
so big that you can't flee from it.

If you nap often during the day you'll
be up all night. So . . . you know . . .
nap often during the day.

Life is short—pet hard.

We enjoy a good movie just as much as the next guy. Just don't put on that *Wizard of Oz*. The way they killed that poor witch at the end with all that water. *Gruesome!*

Contrary to popular belief, staring out the window for hours on end is not a waste of time. That's how I came up with this book.

You can't always get what you want.
Literally. *You* can't always get what
you want. Cats get what they want
pretty much all the time.

It's good to be the cat.

ABOUT ANTHONY RUBINO JR

Tony was raised by a kindle of feral, hypoallergenic, hairless sphinx cats until forced to leave because the cats were allergic to Tony and they were coughing up balls of *his* fur.

Accustomed to hair, an Italian family in New Jersey felt sorry for the young cat-boy and took him in. But he—once again—found himself on the street shortly after refusing a second helping of pasta fagioli. Fortunately, by then he was thirty-five.

Shunned by both cat and human societies, Tony began to look inward and embarked on a quest for knowledge through the careful study of drivel. Never a stickler for math, Tony wrote *Life Lessons from Your Cat* as the fifth installment of his Life-Lessons trilogy, which includes *Life Lessons from Your Dog, Life Lessons from Elvis, Life Lessons from the Bradys,* and *Life Lessons from Melrose Place.* Before that he began his scholarly pursuits by penning *1001 Reasons to Procrastinate.* He's also contributed his articles and cartoons to publications such as: *MAD Magazine, National Lampoon,* the *Chicago Tribune,* and *Opium Magazine.*

His cartoon syndication credits include national distribution by King Features, Tribune Media Services, and Creators Syndicate.

Tony's designs, cartoons, and words can be found on greeting cards and other product lines such as calendars, posters, and apparel sold in stores and catalogs worldwide.

When he's not goofing off with that stuff, you can find him living and working in New York City as a creative director and art director for the advertising and marketing industry—or watching TV.

Despite his repeated attempts to reconcile with his families, they continue to refuse his letters. He suspects it's because the cats can't read and the Italians hold grudges. Or vice versa.

Visit www.rubinocreative.com for more information and big fun.